D1399212

LEARNING ABOUT THE EARTH

Rain Forests

by Colleen Sexton

BLASTOFF! READERS 3

BELLWETHER MEDIA · MINNEAPOLIS, MN

Note to Librarians, Teachers, and Parents:

Blastoff! Readers are carefully developed by literacy experts and combine standards-based content with developmentally-appropriate text.

Level 1 provides the most support through repetition of high-frequency words, light text, predictable sentence patterns, and strong visual support.

Level 2 offers early readers a bit more challenge through varied simple sentences, increased text load, and less repetition of high frequency words.

Level 3 advances early-fluent readers toward fluency through increased text and concept load, less reliance on visuals, longer sentences, and more literary language.

Level 4 builds reading stamina by providing more text per page, increased use of punctuation, greater variation in sentence patterns, and increasingly challenging vocabulary.

Level 5 encourages children to move from "learning to read" to "reading to learn" by providing even more text, varied writing styles, and less familiar topics.

Whichever book is right for your reader, Blastoff! Readers are the perfect books to build confidence and encourage a love of reading that will last a lifetime!

This edition first published in 2008 by Bellwether Media.

No part of this publication may be reproduced in whole or in part without written permission of the publisher. For information regarding permission, write to Bellwether Media Inc., Attention: Permissions Department, Post Office Box 1C, Minnetonka, MN 55345-9998.

Library of Congress Cataloging-in-Publication Data
Sexton, Colleen A., 1967–
  Rain forests / by Colleen Sexton.
    p. cm. – (Blastoff! readers. Learning about the earth)
Summary: "Simple text and supportive images introduce beginning readers to the physical characteristics and geographic locations of Rain Forests"–Provided by publisher.
  Includes bibliographical references and index.
  ISBN-13: 978-1-60014-115-7 (hardcover : alk. paper)
  ISBN-10: 1-60014-115-3 (hardcover : alk. paper)
  1. Rain forests–Juvenile literature. 2. Rain forest ecology–Juvenile literature. I. Title.

QH86.S49 2008
578.734–dc22   2007014942

Contents

What Are Rain Forests?   4

Rain Forest Layers   9

Plants and Animals   14

Rain Forests and People   19

Glossary   22

To Learn More   23

Index   24

Rain forests are thick jungles with tall trees. More than 80 inches (203 centimeters) of rain falls in rain forests every year.

Some rain forests get as much as 260 inches (660 centimeters) of rain per year!

Most rain forests grow in the **tropics**. This area circles the middle of the earth like a belt.

6

Rain forests in the tropics are hot and damp. In some places it rains 200 days a year.

Rivers flow through
rain forests. They carry
rainwater to the ocean.

Tropical rain forests grow in
layers. The **canopy** is at the top.
The leaves and branches of tall
trees form a roof over the forest.

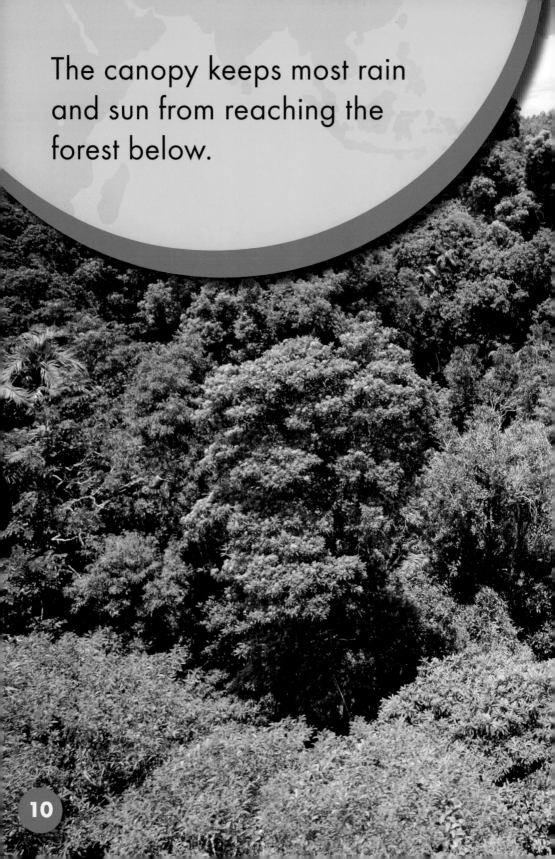

The canopy keeps most rain and sun from reaching the forest below.

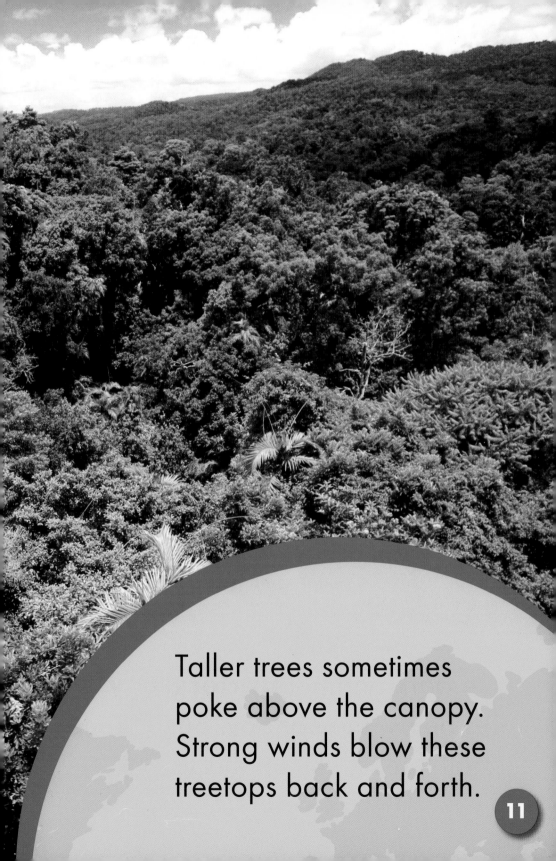

Taller trees sometimes poke above the canopy. Strong winds blow these treetops back and forth.

The dark and hot **understory** lies below the canopy. Bushes and small trees make up this layer.

Fallen leaves, branches, and seeds cover the forest floor. Huge tree roots grow across the ground.

The rain and heat of the tropics make rain forests grow thick with plants. Vines climb up tree trunks. Flowers grow in the sunny treetops.

Some plants grow wide
leaves to catch rain.

Tropical rain forests are home
to more than half of the world's
animals. Crocodiles and
snakes live near rivers.

Monkeys leap from branch to branch in the canopy. Jaguars creep through the understory.

Parrots, toucans, and other
colorful birds fly in the treetops.

Tropical rain forests are an important **resource** for people. Fruits, spices, nuts, and other food comes from rain forests. Scientists make medicines from rain forest plants.

Some people take too many resources from the rain forest. This hurts rain forest life.

Many groups are working to save rain forests. They want to protect the plants and animals that live there.

Glossary

canopy—a thick covering of leafy branches formed by the tops of trees

resource—something that has value or is useful

tropics—the hot and wet area near the equator

understory—the layer below the canopy made up of small trees and bushes

To Learn More

AT THE LIBRARY

Berkes, Marianne. *Over in the Jungle: A Rainforest Rhyme*. Nevada City, Calif.: Dawn Publications, 2007.

Canizares, Susan. *Rainforest Colors*. New York: Scholastic, 1998.

Cherry, Lynne. *The Great Kapok Tree: A Tale of the Amazon Rain Forest*. San Diego, Calif.: Harcourt Brace Jovanovich, 1990.

Dunphy, Madeleine. *Here Is the Tropical Rain Forest*. New York: Hyperion Books for Children, 1994.

Gibbons, Gail. *Nature's Green Umbrella: Tropical Rain Forests*. New York: Morrow Junior Books, 1994.

Yolen, Jane. *Welcome to the Green House*. New York: Putnam, 1993.

ON THE WEB
Learning more about rain forests is as easy as 1, 2, 3.

1. Go to www.factsurfer.com

2. Enter "rain forests" into search box.

3. Click the "Surf" button and you will see a list of related web sites.

With factsurfer.com, finding more information is just a click away.

Index

animals, 16, 21
birds, 18
branches, 9, 13, 17
bushes, 12
canopy, 9, 10, 11, 12, 17
earth, 6
floor, 13
flowers, 14
food, 19
heat, 14
jaguars, 17
jungle, 4
layers, 9, 12
leaves, 9, 13, 15
medicine, 19
monkeys, 17
ocean, 8
parrots, 18
people, 19, 20
plants, 14, 15, 19, 21
rain, 4, 5, 7, 10, 14, 15
rainwater, 8
resource, 19, 20

rivers, 8, 16
roots, 13
seeds, 13
sun, 10
toucans, 18
trees, 4, 9, 11, 12
treetops, 11, 14, 18
tropics, 6, 7, 14
trunks, 14
understory, 12, 17
vines, 14
winds, 11

The photographs in this book are reproduced through the courtesy of: Robyn Mackenzie, front cover, pp. 6-7; Gail Shumway/Getty Images, pp. 4-5; Johnny Lye, p. 8; Finn O'Hara, p. 9; Tim Graham/Getty Images, pp. 10-11; Carlos S. Pereyra/agefotostock, p. 12; Paul Cowan, p. 13; Roland Ackermann, p. 14; Nitpong Ballapavanich, p. 15; Jack Milchanowski/agefotostock, p. 16; National Geographic/Getty Images, p. 17; Arco/P. Wgner/agefotostock, p. 18; Ricardo Beliel/BrazilPhotos/Alamy, p. 19, Jeremy Walker/Getty Images, pp. 20-21.